Introducti

This little book of recipes is written to not just help people with their recipe ideas and how to use Sea Vegetables better, but also to introduce some healthier options for some favourite foods. I cook at home for my family on an almost daily basis, so all the recipes here have been made at home in my small and cluttered kitchen, for myself and my family. The aim is to promote healthy food, and wholesome food which just tastes good.

The first part of the book is about Sea Vegetables, with their nutritional data sheets, and suggested uses.

The middle section of the book is for "Street Food" or party food to cook at home to serve lots of people.

The final part of this book is full of cakes. This is because we love to eat cake, and too much cake is too unhealthy. Starting from how to use Carrageen in vegan cakes, and making vegan cakes with carrageen for a vegan fair in Edinburgh, I explored how to make my cakes healthier, and tastier because cake is to be enjoyed and loved, and no-one should be excluded from our cake culture. I have tried to eliminate the most harmful ingredients from my cakes and include the healthier alternatives.

Seaweed and Oatcakes

Published by SeaVeg Publishing in 2017
55 Wallace Crescent. Roslin. EH25 9LN

First Edition October 2017

ISBN   978-1-5272-1444-6

Produced using LibreOffice on x86 Linux

Printed and bound in the UK by Biddles Books Ltd.

Table of Contents

Seaweed and Oatcakes

Royal Presentation 2015

This was the presentation table of **"Seaweed and Oatcakes"** prepared by Debra Riddell at Breadshare Bakery in Portobello for the visit by HRH The Duchess of Rothesay.

Seaweed and Oatcakes

Dulse: Palmaria palmata

Dulse has always been one of the most popular sea vegetables. It is dark red in colour and can be found all round the coastal areas of the northern hemisphere above 50 degrees North or where the sea has a typical ambient temperature of below 14C, growing on rocks below the low water mark, and on other larger seaweeds such as kelps and wracks. There are numerous unregistered health claims made about dulse which are attributed to its wealth of available minerals which include notably Iodine, Potassium, Manganese, and Iron, and vitamins which include Vitamin A, and Vitamin B12 in significant amounts and others in much smaller quantities. This book is about culinary use and anyone wishing to use SeaVeg as a medicinal herb should consult a qualified professional. It should be noted that 8g of dulse contains typically 15 x the recommended daily intake of Iodine which may in itself cause health issues if consumed in excess. The French seaweed institute CEVA has published aggregate data on nutritional content of edible algae, and from their data tables the following "typical" values can be obtained though there are wide seasonal variations:

Typical nutritional data based on CEVA data is for dried seaweed.

Seaweed and Oatcakes

Nutrition Information
Irish Dulse – palmaria palmata

Typical Values		Per 100g	Per 8g serving	% RI per 8g serving	RI Adult
Energy	Kj	703	56	0.67	8400
	kcal	168	13		2000
Fat (g)		1.4	0.1	0.14	70
Saturates (g)		0.34	0.03	0.14	20
Carbohydrate (g)		21.8	1.7	0.65	260
Sugars (g)		0	0		90
Fibre (g)		29	2.3		
Protein (g)		17	1.4	2.8	50
Salt (g)		3.9	0.3	5	6
Vitamins and Minerals			Per 8g	%NRV	NRV
Vitamin A (ug)		3732	298	37	800
Vitamin B12 (ug)		10	0.8	32	2.5
Vitamin C (mg)		84	6.7	8	80
Copper (mg)		0.9	0.07	7	1
Manganese (mg)		11	0.88	45	2
Iodine (ug)		28900	2312	1541	150
Potassium (g)		7	0.6	12	4.7

RI = Reference intake of an average adult (8 400 kJ/2 000 kcal)

Food supplements should not be used as a substitute for a varied diet.
Source CEVA aggregated data

Dulse is classed as a "Food Supplement" in the EU.

Seaweed and Oatcakes

The presence of significant vitamin B12 makes this an important component for a vegan diet, though care should be used to remove any small brine shrimp or other marine creatures which may be found attached to the seaweed before serving or further processing. There is also a high risk of cross contamination with molluscs and crustacea which naturally inhabit the seaweed in the wild, and those with severe allergies should probably avoid unprocessed seaweeds altogether.

Dulse is traditionally harvested with care, and it is not the intention to harvest any marine creatures, and those who object to finding such small critters in their food should probably consider how industrially produced commercial food can be delivered entirely without any traces of the natural abundance of small insects which inhabit our planet. This is often achieved by chemical mass extermination and I would not want to see this being done in a marine environment.

Dulse has been consumed traditionally in many coastal areas of western Europe, and is often eaten as a salty snack. There is an abundance of small harvesting operations along the west coast of Ireland, as well as Greenland and Iceland, and it can often be found in grocers shops alongside sacks of potatoes which it complements well.

Seaweed and Oatcakes

Flaked dulse can be sprinkled on top of cooked (steamed) potatoes just before serving to add a delicious flavour to complement the dish.

Dulse drying at Quality SeaVeg in Donegal

Our Potato Scones with dulse flakes can be made with leftover mashed potato and are delicious with breakfast.

Potato Scones with Dulse Flakes

Using leftover mashed potato, add one third of the weight of potato, of white or wholemeal spelt or other flour, and a handful of flaked dulse, knead together and press into flat cakes, put a little oil into a pan and cook 6 mins a side on a moderate heat. Bake in medium oven (140C) for a further 20 mins.

Extra special when reheated in the oven later.

Seaweed and Oatcakes

Irish Sea Spaghetti: Himanthalia elongata

This is a seaweed with a two year life cycle. In the first year it grows buttons from its spores, and in the second year it grows long tendrils which are the fruiting body. It is these tendrils which are knows as "Sea Spaghetti"

Sea Spaghetti grows all round the British Isles on rocks accessible at low tide.

Seaweed and Oatcakes

Typical Nutrition for dried sea spaghetti.

Typical Values		Per 100g	Per 8g serving	% RI per 8g serving	RI Adult
Nutrition Information					
Irish Sea Spaghetti – Himanthalia Elongata					
Energy	Kj	747	60	2.34	8400
	kcal	178	14		2000
Fat		2.7	0.22	0.31	70
Saturates		0.7	0.06	0.3	20
Carbohydrate		28.5	2.3	0.88	260
Sugars		0	0		90
Fibre		30.5	2.4		
Protein		10	0.8	1.48	50
Salt		9.0	0.7	12	6
Vitamins and Minerals					
Vitamin A (ug)		253	20	2.5	800
Vitamin B2 (mg)		4.5	0.36	25	1.4
Vitamin C (mg)		66	5	6.25	80
Vitamin E (mg)		5.8	0.5	4	12
Magnesium (mg)		1590	127	34	375
Iodine (ug)		14600	1168	779	150
Zinc (mg)		40	3	30	10

Based on CEVA aggregated data

Irish Sea Spaghetti can be considered to be a useful source of Iodine, Magnesium, Zinc, and vitamin B2.

Seaweed and Oatcakes

Before use, dried sea spaghetti should be quickly washed in cold water. If you want to make a cold dashi stock, then soak the sea spaghetti for at least 10 minutes.

Soup made from Sea Spaghetti Dashi with herbs.

Sea spaghetti cooks best when accompanied by some kind of citrus, any citrus will do, but I prefer Lemons and Limes, choose organic or unwaxed fruit otherwise you will be adding potentially toxic hydrocarbons to your cooking. Dashi is a Japanese stock made from seaweed.

Seaweed and Oatcakes

Irish Spirulina (Atlantic Greens) is a green seaweed, commonly called "gutweed" and recently reclassified from Enteromorpha spirulina to Ulva spiralis. It can be found in rock pools, and where freshwater runs into the sea.

It will go sticky quickly if roasted, but is excellent in clear soups just add to bouillon and serve immediately. Cooks well with rice in a rice cooker.

Steamed Carrots with Irish Spirulina

Seaweed and Oatcakes

Nutrition Information
Irish Spirulina - Ulva spiralis

Typical Values		Per 100g	Per 8g serving	% RI per 8g serving	RI Adult
Energy	Kj	605	48	0.6	8400
	kcal	144	11.5		
Fat (g)		3	0.24	0.3	70
Saturates		0.7	0.1	0.3	20
Carbohydrate		17	1.3	0.5	260
Sugars		0	0		
Fibre (g)		33	2.6		
Protein (g)		12	1	2	50
Salt (g)		13	1	17	6
Vitamins and Minerals					
Vitamin A (ug)		1000	80	10	800
Vitamin B12 (ug)		30	2.3	93	2.5
Vitamin C (mg)		35	2.8	3.5	80
Copper (ug)		1200	96	9.6	1000
Manganese (mg)		12	1	50	2
Iodine (ug)		9200	736	490	150
Phosphorous (mg)		1150	92	13	700

Based on CEVA aggregated data.

When quite simply used as a garnish and to decorate, our Irish Spirulina adds colour and variety to a family favourite. It has an abundance of vitamin B12, is rich in Manganese and has plenty but not too excessive Iodine.

Seaweed and Oatcakes

The Kelps – Laminaria Digitata, and Saccharina Latissima.

Current advice is that these should not actually be eaten on a regular basis due to the very high Iodine content, but small amounts used as seasoning's, flavourings, and for their mineral content including cooking chemistry are acceptable.

Sugar Kelp (L. Saccharina) has 366mg/100g aggregated iodine, and Kombu (L.digitata) has 433 mg/100g according to data published by the French seaweed institute at www.ceva.fr. The recommended daily reference intake of Iodine is 150 microgram, so 1g of kelp will contain up to 4mg of Iodine which can be up to 25 times the recommended daily intake. The kombu is used in the "Ocean Seasons" range of seaweed seasoning, and the sugar kelp is used in the mixed seaveg, and salad flakes shaker pots. In Japan the kombu is used to make dashi, and in other Asian countries the seaweed is removed from dishes before serving as being used only to aid the cooking process.

Kombu (Laminaria Digitata) and Sugar Kelp (Saccharina Latissima/Laminaria Saccharina) are both classed as a Food in the EU, but should be consumed with caution.

Seaweed and Oatcakes

Purple Laver is a thin seaweed often found on rocks which are exposed at low tide. Its common name is "sloke" and its botanical classification is "Porphyra umbellicalis". It is best picked in late winter when it is dark blackish purple, in early summer it becomes greenish purple to dark green.

Purple laver can be eaten raw, or used as a garnish. Peel and chop some parsnips, and add some whole peeled garlic, pour over some olive oil and roast for 10-15 minutes, then when still hot add some purple laver, stir and serve immediately.

Roasted Parsnips with Purple Laver

Seaweed and Oatcakes

Purple laver is particularly rich in vitamin B12, and also contains significant vitamin A, manganese, and iodine, and unlike many other seaweeds and the iodine content is not excessive.

Nutrition Information
Irish Purple Laver

Typical Values	Per 100g	Per 8g serving		Adult RI
		g	%RI	
Energy Kj	739	59	0.7	8400
kcal	176	14		2000
Fat (g)	1.6	0.13	0.18	70
Saturates	0.4	0.03	0.16	20
Carbohydrate	13	1	0.4	260
Sugars	0	0		
Fibre (g)	34	2.7		
Protein (g)	27.5	2.2	4.4	50
Salt (g)	4.8	0.38	6.4	6
Vitamins and Minerals			%NRV	NRV
Vitamin A (ug)	4470	357	45	800
Vitamin B12 (ug)	44	3.5	140	2.5
Vitamin C (mg)	62	5	6	80
Copper (mg)	0.7	0.06	5	1
Manganese (mg)	424	34	1700	2
Iodine (ug)	2500	200	133	150
Potassium (g)	1.4	0.1	5	2
Phosphorous (mg)	446	36	5	700

Nutrition Information based on CEVA published aggregated data.

Carrageen

Carrageen is a red seaweed, which is hung outdoors for several weeks to be washed by the rain and bleached by the sun before use

Irish Carrageen hanging outside to bleach and wash at Quality SeaVeg in Donegal.

Seaweed and Oatcakes

Preparing Carrageen Jelly

Put 6g of carrageen into a pan with 300g water, allow to stand for 30 mins remove any stems twigs etc. and boil for 2-3 minutes, stirring all the time, then turn down the heat and simmer for 20 mins to allow the mixture to break down and thicken, remove from heat and allow to cool. The mass should be reduced to about 100g or about a third of its original volume. This is used later in some cake recipes or as a thickener.

Seaweed and Oatcakes

Carrageen is used primarily as a thickener, and gelling agent.

Nutrition Information				
Irish Carragheen				
Typical Values	Per 100g	Per 2g serving		RI Adult
		g	% RI	
Energy Kj	774	15	0.2	8400
Kcal	185	3.7		2000
Fat	2.5	0.05	0.07	70
Saturated	0.13	0		
Carbohydrate	25	0.5	0.2	260
Sugar	0			
Protein	16	0.32	0.6	50
Salt (g)	9.5	0.2	3	6
Minerals			% of NRV	
Magnesium (mg)	1260	25	6.7	375
Iron (mg)	19.3	0.4	3	14
Iodine (ug)	34200	684	456	150
Potassium (mg)	4600	92	4.6	2000
Zinc (mg)	77	1.5	15	10

Based on CEVA aggregated data

Carrageen is a good natural source of Iodine as it is not in too great a concentration with typical consumption in a prepared food being less than 1g.

Thick Hot Chocolate with Irish Carrageen

Wash and put 7g (a ¼ oz) of SeaVeg Irish Carrageen into a pan with a litre of any vegan alternative "Milk" such as soya, Almond, Oat or Cashew "Milk". Add sugar and cocoa to taste, Bring to boil and boil for 7-10 minutes, stirring all the time to thicken. Pour through a sieve and serve.

This can be set in the fridge to make a delicious chocolate pudding.

Chocolate Carrageen Pudding

If using home made nut "Milk" cook the carrageen separately in water, and then add the mix to the blender.

Seaweed and Oatcakes

Home Made Oatcakes (with Seaweed)

This was one of my first recipes, I use rolled oats, or jumbo oats. It is best if you use Organic oats and support farmers who do not exterminate the hedgerow wildlife by spraying their crops with poisons.

Oatcakes with Purple Laver

Seaweed and Oatcakes

Put 200g porridge oats and 8-10g chopped seaweed into your blender, and blend till it becomes a fine floury mix.

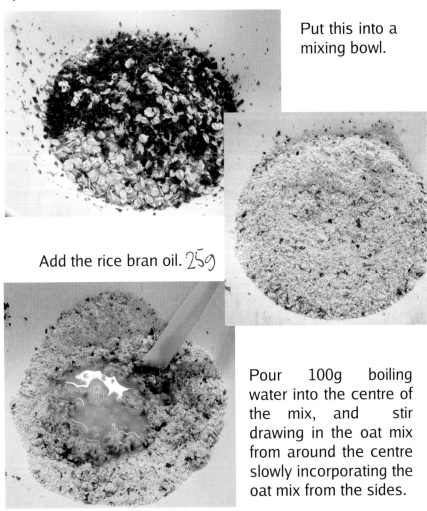

Put this into a mixing bowl.

Add the rice bran oil. 25g

Pour 100g boiling water into the centre of the mix, and stir drawing in the oat mix from around the centre slowly incorporating the oat mix from the sides.

Seaweed and Oatcakes

You should end up with a stiff dough which does not crack too much when you roll it out.

Put the oven on to 160C, and clear a space for rolling. It is easier to roll a few at a time, so get your cutter of choice, and take a handful of dough, and press it into a rough oatcake shape, then roll it into about 5-6mm thick before trimming with a cutter, and put these onto a dry baking paper lined baking sheet, bake for 40 mins at 160C or until light golden brown.

Oatcakes will keep for up to a few weeks in a sealed container, maybe a little longer.

Street Food at home.

This section is dedicated to easy to cook at home recipes, perfect for parties.

Tofu with Flaked Mixed SeaVeg.

Tofu is gently cooked in a pan with toasted sesame oil, add a little dark soy sauce, and the juice of half a lemon, and cook till it starts to brown, then sprinkled with mixed seaveg flakes and serve.

Seaweed and Oatcakes

Pizza Base

Pizza is very easy to make at home, and tastes much better than shop or takeaway pizza. Prepare your yeast mix to 300g fluid and put in a warm place. Take a half bag (500g) of "Malthouse" flour. Again organic flours are better because there is much less harm to the environment, and without added preservatives it should taste better too, I sieve the flour to remove the added grains leaving about 450g. You can use these later either in bread or for bird feed. Snails also love them and if you want to keep the snails off your salads, put them in a tray near your beds. Put the sieved flour into a mixing bowl. There is no need to add salt to the dough, but you may add some seaweed seasoning, fine chopped seaweed or other herbs at this stage. Add about 30g of good olive or other edible oil and mix gently, pour the yeast mix into the middle of the bowl, and begin stirring in the mix from the middle, and allowing the flour to fall in to the middle from the sides to make a ball. As you mix you will see the gluten strands forming, the dough should remain soft and form a ball.

Put this aside for 30 mins whilst you prepare toppings.

Line your tins with paper, it really is better for not having your pizza stuck to a tin, and don't use any oil at all.

Seaweed and Oatcakes

Divide the dough into half, and form into soft balls. Spread these out by hand, you may have seen experts spinning their pizza base by hand. Your dough should be soft and springy, so feel free to give it a try. Failing that push the dough into your desired shape in the tins.

Make your tomato paste by using up any overripe tomatoes. Chop these and add to your smoothie maker together with some tomato puree, and a few cloves of peeled garlic, blend till smooth, and sieve into a jug before using. Alternatively you can use shop bought passata, chopped tomatoes, garlic paste etc. Add any fresh herbs to taste. Peppers and mushrooms always make good toppings, as do red onions, chopped seaweed, and maybe even nuts.

Bake at 200C for 10 - 15 mins approx.

Seaweed and Oatcakes

SeaVeg Burgers - makes 8 x 115g burgers

Grate 2 carrots (150g) and
2 medium beetroot (200g), add to a pan with a
1/2 cup green lentils (100g), sprouted in advance (250g).
1/2 cup SeaVeg SeaSpice or mixed Seaveg flakes (14g),
1 heaped teaspoon SeaVeg carrageen flakes (4g),

Here you can add any flavours you like such as garam masala, ground cumin, garlic etc., then add 3 cups water, bring to boil and simmer for 40 minutes. When cooked remove from heat drain off excess fluid using a sieve, and slowly stir in gram flour to bind (I used up to 300g). It is best to have plenty of gram flour handy when forming burgers as it helps stop the mix sticking to your hands. Re-fry for 10-12 mins turning occasionally. Often I use 2 large serving spoons, and spoon the mix directly into the pan to form patties. These can be cooked as a batch, kept in the fridge for a few days, or frozen as necessary, but if you freeze them defrost properly before cooking.

These are delicious cold, and when served with well known brands of Indian pickles. You can season these with herbs and spices to your own taste. I have used fresh ground cumin when cooking, fresh garden herbs when forming into burgers, or stir in freshly sprouted lentils when forming the burgers for added crunch.

Seaweed and Oatcakes

If you make the burgers by hand, you will probably make them too thick. In which case you will need to put them in the oven after frying. To cook them a little more put them is the oven for maybe 20 mins at 140C. If you have made a big batch for a barbeque then you will want them to be ready in advance anyway.

SeaVeg burger Served with a salsa of fresh tomatoes and chopped purple laver.

Curry Base

Home made Curry: There are numerous ways to make curry bases, but generally they all start with the same few basic ingredients – Onions, Garlic, Cumin seeds, Coriander seeds.

First finely chop an onion – or two and put into a pan on a low heat with a little oil, add the garlic and cook gently till the onions have softened and started to brown. If you get any signs of spitting or smoke then you are cooking too hot, so turn it down. If you are cooking lots of different things, then you can put all the onions and garlic together, and cook in advance, then take what you need for individual dishes. Freshly ground cumin and coriander are generally added to all curry bases as these spices are beneficial for the digestive system.

Korma style base is made by adding finely grated ginger and turmeric to the onion garlic base, and later adding almonds and almond milk.

Jalfrezi style base is made by adding tomato passata, and "Garam Masala" which means mixed spices – Garam is flavour, Masala is mixture.

There is a wide variety of other flavours which can be made by a combination of generally two other spices.

Sprouted Lentils – green lentils are great sprouted, take about a cup – 100g of organic green lentils, put them into a jar and add about a pint of water water. Cover and leave till the next day, then drain, rinse and cover. After 1 day the lentils can be used in recipes cooked, the following few days they can also be used in recipes, and after about 5 days they will have sprouted and can just be eaten in salads.

Mild Green Dahl - serves 4

This is a favourite at home, and quick and easy to make.
First prepare the onions and garlic as described under curry base. Add to this some finely grated ginger and turmeric. When the onions are ready chop 1 courgette and add it to the pan, then add some freshly ground cumin and coriander seeds. Other vegetables can of course be added with the courgette, my family like mushrooms and aubergines. Cover this and cook slowly till the courgette has softened and other vegetables cooked.
Whilst the courgette is cooking, put some soaked or sprouted green lentils into the pressure cooker, and cook for 12 to 15 minutes, allow to decompress naturally.
When the pressure is released, drain and add the lentils to the curry pan, stir, add some home made almond milk and almond milk paste. Stir and serve.

Southern Beans – serves 4

This is a favourite bean recipe, it uses american black – or southern beans. Prepare the beans first by adding 600ml of cold water to 200g dried black beans, and allow to soak for 24 hrs. Rinse and drain before use.
Pressure cook the beans for 15 mins, and allow to decompress and cool naturally.

Prepare a base using onions and garlic as described in the curry base recipe, and when the onions are cooked add the beans, and a 750g carton or bottle of passata, a tablespoon of spanish paprika, and some chopped red peppers. Chilli is optional but my family don't like it hot.

Cover the pan and cook on a gentle heat for another 20 mins or until the peppers have softened. Sweeten with ground sweet cinnamon.

Serve with Rice, bread, corn chips etc. to suit.

Sweet Potatoes and Red Cabbage

I often make this at the same time as the SeaKraut, put some olive oil into a pan on a medium heat, and add a handful of cumin seeds, and some chopped garlic. Slice in the sweet potato, and cover the sweet potato with chopped red cabbage. Put a lid on the pan and cook slowly for 20-30 mins making sure that it does not burn. The sweet potato will gently brown on the bottom, and the red cabbage will steam above it.

Seaweed and Oatcakes

SeaKraut – sauerkraut with sea salt and seaweed

I use red cabbage for this, finely grate the cabbage into a bowl, add a handful of sea salt, and a handful of flaked Irish Dulse and mix well, put this into a sterilised jar – I use a spare smoothie jug – and press down well, cover with a spare cabbage leaf, and put the lid on making sure that its not airtight. Top up with a little cooled boiled water from the kettle. Put in a warm dark corner of the kitchen for 3-4 days minimum, let the pressure out of the jug occasionally.

This can be eaten raw, or cooked gently before serving. If you find it too salty, add cooled boiled water from the kettle before serving, drain and add a little Cider vinegar, or Balsamic vinegar.

How Now No Cow !

"Milk"s can be made from a variety of nuts and grains.

Home Made Almond Milk

Seaweed and Oatcakes

Almond Milk

Ingredients: 100g whole almonds, 1l Water.

To make 1l of good home made almond milk.

Take 100g fresh whole almonds, put them into a jar and add 500ml cold water, allow to stand for between 8 and 24 hrs. The maximum time for soaking is 48 hrs approx, and the minimum is 8 hrs. If you soak for too long they will become bitter. I use a section cut from some polyester net curtains as a filter, it can be washed after use. Drain the soaked almonds and put them into a pan. You don't absolutely have to soak the almonds, but its better if you do as the process helps with enzyme production as they start to sprout.

Blanch the almonds by pouring over boiling water, and allow to stand for a minute or two. The skins will soften and be easier to remove. Remove and discard the almond skins, and place the skinned almonds into a blender cup. You will get about 140 g of soaked shelled almonds. Add 600ml water, and blend till smooth.

Put a sieve over 1l pyrex jug and a square of the clean net curtain fabric over the sieve, and pour the mixture from the blender into the strainer. When it has dripped through. Return the remaining almond paste to the blender jug, and add another 500ml cold water. Repeat the blend and straining process.

Seaweed and Oatcakes

If you like you can do the blend and strain a third time, but you will have a less full milk, generally I just do the blend and sieve twice. The fresh almond milk should be stored in the fridge, and used within 2-3 days. Keep the almond milk "paste" which is left over, this can be used in other recipes too.

Oat Milk is made in a similar way using whole Oat Grains – called groats. Soak the whole Oat grains for 8 hours before blending. Put the oats and soak water into the blender together. Blend till smooth and strain through the net curtain sieve. Return the residual grain to the blender and add another 500ml water. Blend till smooth, and strain, pouring the strained fluid into a litre jug or bottle. Oat milk will keep for 2 days in the fridge, otherwise use same day. It will ferment if left out.

Cashew Milk Cashew nuts need no soaking, just put 100g of unroasted cashews into the blender jug, add 600ml cold water and blend. Strain as before and return the residual nut paste to the blender, add another 500ml cold water and blend again and strain as before.

Vegan pancake or batter mix

The batter mix follows the almond milk, because you need the almond milk or Oat Milk for the batter, or you can use the remaining almond paste

120g silken Tofu
160g white spelt
200ml almond or other nut or Oat milk
Teaspoon baking powder.

If you are using almond paste from making almond milk, add 200g water.

Blend together all the ingredients, and allow to stand for 2-3 minutes whilst you get the pan hot.

Pour a little oil – I use Rice Bran Oil, but you may have your own favourite – into the pan, and wait till its hot before pouring some of the batter mix in to fry. The first pancake is typically wrong, but it lets you know when the pan is hot as it will be cooked. If you use a ladle to measure your mix you will get consistent pancakes.
For each pancake, pour a little oil into the pan and swirl it round before addinb a ladle of batter mix to the pan, allow to cook through before turning.

Serve with conserve or lemon to taste.

Healthy Cakes

or

"where there is cake there is hope."

This "half" of the book is dedicated entirely to vegan cake recipes, all of which have been the results of many months of experiments in my own kitchen.

In the beginning I made the first cakes using Irish Carrageen. This allowed me to make cake with polenta, so the first two recipes are "Ginger and Apricot Polenta Cake", and "Rhubarb and Ginger polenta cake" both of which use French made conserve instead of adding both fruit and sugar. If you make them without carrageen the cake may harden due to the nature of polenta.

The next section of cakes are those which use bananas as a base with ground almonds, though one has no almonds for those who cannot have them. Then we have cakes using barley flour, and a cake which uses barley flour and no bananas or nuts.

Finally we use Tofu as the cake base, to which, as it makes a very soft sponge, we add other flours to compensate.

In general I have tried to keep the sugar content as low as practicable, typically to below 20% total sugar content.

Seaweed and Oatcakes

Apricot and Ginger Polenta Cake

(Rhubarb and ginger polenta cake)
100g Carrageen Jelly
30g rice bran oil
200g apricot or rhubarb conserve
50g stem ginger + 50g syrup from the jar
150g fine polenta

Prepare the carrageen jelly as described in the section under Irish Carrageen. Put into a blender together with the rice bran oil, the stem ginger and syrup, and half the conserve, and 50g cold water and blend till smooth. Pour this into the mixing bowl and add the remaining conserve, 150g polenta and 10g of bicarbonate of soda and mix well. The mixture should be soft. If it's too stiff add a little more water. Line your baking tin with parchment paper, and pour in the mixture, bake at 150C for 30 mins.

To finish, glaze with some more apricot conserve.

If you make the polenta cake without carrageen it is likely to harden overnight and lose its soft texture.

For Rhubarb and Ginger Polenta cake use Rhubarb conserve instead of Apricot conserve.

Seaweed and Oatcakes

Apricot and Ginger polenta cake

Banana and Ground Almond Cake

200g Banana,
40g Rice Bran Oil,
100g ground almonds,
100g sugar,
150g white spelt flour,
10g baking powder

Add the bananas, almonds, sugar and oil to mixing bowl, mash and mix well (optional vanilla). You can use a blender or smoothie maker to do the mixing if you like.

Add the white spelt flour and 2 teaspoons of baking powder, and mix well. The mixture should be soft and not too stiff, so if the bananas are not fully ripe you may need to add a tablespoon of water to soften the mix. Line a 10 inch cake tin with paper, pour mix into tin and bake at 160C for 30 mins.

If you try to scale the recipe up too much, baking time will increase, and it may sink in the middle. If the dough is too stiff it may not have the right texture

For a great variation, add 70g dark chocolate to the blender, and use just 80g sugar and 30g Rice Bran Oil.

To make the cake without almonds just miss them out of the mix, and maybe add a little vanilla bean paste instead. Try this recipe for Banana Muffins.

Banana Muffins

These use coconut flour instead of ground almonds

260g ripe banana
100g sugar
160g white spelt
40 g Rice Bran Oil
20g Coconut Flour
10g Vanilla Bean Paste
10g baking powder

Blend all the ingredients except the flour and baking powder together, put the flour and baking powder into a mixing bowl and mix well.

The coconut flour is optional, it makes a thicker mix.

Pour in the mixture from the blender, and mix together well, put into muffin cases (makes 8) and bake 20 mins at 175C

Chocolate Date and Walnut Cake

This cake is made entirely without added sugar, but there is 66% sugar content in the date syrup, and 24% sugar content in the dark chocolate which means it has about 20% overall sugar content.

Seaweed and Oatcakes

Ingredients:

200g Ripe Banana
100g Ground Almonds
100g Date Syrup
50g Dark Chocolate
50g Walnuts
40g Rice Bran Oil
10g Baking powder
150g White Spelt
30g water

Mash the bananas, and add them together with the ground almonds, date syrup, Dark Chocolate, Oil, water, and Walnuts into a blender and blend till smooth, then add to a mixing bowl, together with the baking powder and white spelt flour. Mix together and put into a lined 9 inch cake tin and bake for 25 to 30 mins at 160C.
The total sugar in this cake is 40g from the bananas, 66g from date syrup, and 12g from the chocolate. Total sugars 118g from a 700g mix.

Barley Cake

Barley is a traditional grain which has fallen out of favour in recent times, it may be hard to find, and is known to be difficult to work with as it is quite dense.

The next few recipes are for Barley Cakes which are quite handy if you want to avoid wheat in your cakes.

Lemon Barley Cake

125g Barley flour
100g Carrageen Gel (from 7g carrageen)
100g caster sugar
40g Rice Bran Oil
2 lemons
50g water
8g baking powder.

Seaweed and Oatcakes

Prepare a baking tin with lining paper, and oven to 175C. Put the sugar, carrageen gel, lemon juice and zest from 1 lemon, rice bran oil, and water into the blender, and blend till smooth. Put the barley flour into a bowl, and add the fluid from the blender. Mix well before adding 8g baking powder, mix well again and pour into the baking tin and bake for 30 mins.

The glazing is made from carrageen, sugar, barley flour and lemon. The lemon juice, sugar and zest is added to the pan with the carrageen gel, and a little water and heated till it nearly boils. Then a desert spoon of barley flour is added and the mixture is cooked till it thickens.

Apple Barley Cake

300g fine grated apple
150g Barley flour
40g Rice Bran Oil
teaspoon baking powder

Apple barley cake can be made quickly and easily without added sugar, simply finely grate a few apples, and add half their weight of barley flour, the rice bran oil, and a teaspoon of baking powder, mix well, put into a 16cm baking tin and bake for 25 mins, some cinnamon and spice may be added if desired.

Tamarind and Ginger Barley Cake

"This cake is overflowing with flavour. It has the warmth of cinnamon, the fire from Ginger, and the zing from the tamarind in a harmony which is rarely found."

Making this cake is probably easiest if you put the blender cup directly on the scales, and add ingredients directly into it.

200g ripe banana (that's nearly 3 medium bananas),
130g Jaggery Goor – (soft panela), grated or sliced,
100g stem ginger and
50g syrup from the stem ginger jar.
40g Rice Bran Oil,
8g sweet cinnamon,
8g (1 teaspoon) Suma Tamarind Paste

Add all the above ingredients to a blender jug, Blend until smooth. Pour this mix into a mixing bowl and add 150g barley flour and 10g baking powder, mix well and pour into a paper lined 20cm baking tin, bake for 30 mins at 175C.

If you make this with sugar instead of panela, only use 100g of sugar, and use a light muscovado sugar.

Seaweed and Oatcakes

Tamarind and ginger barley cake

Choco-coconut-Barley Cake

My first attempts at coconut flour cakes were a complete disaster, it was just gloop, but it can make good cakes, it just needs to be better understood. Coconut flour will drink 5 times its own weight in water, but when combined with Barley flour the results are quite good, also in the muffins the coconut flour took the place of 100g ground Almonds.

200g ripe banana
100g caster sugar
30g Coconut Flour or 100g ground almonds
40g Rice Bran Oil
50g cocoa powder
120g barley flour
50g water
10g baking powder

Add the banana, oil, sugar, water, and cocoa powder to the blender and blend till smooth. Put the barley and coconut flour (or ground almonds) and baking powder into a bowl and mix, pour the mix from the blender into the bowl and mix well.

Seaweed and Oatcakes

This chocolate almond barley cake was made as before, but with 100g ground almonds instead of coconut flour.

Chocolate Almond Barley Cake

Choc Banana Muffins

300g ripe banana.
80g caster sugar
40g Rice Bran Oil
60g Dark chocolate

Put all the above ingredients into a blender, and blend till smooth. Put 200g white spelt flour, and 10g baking powder into a mixing bowl and mix together, add the banana mix from the blender and mix together.

Spoon the mix into bun cases in a tray, and bake at 175C for 20 mins.

Seaweed and Oatcakes

Tofu is another ingredient which can be used in cakes instead of eggs. It also helps the fluid content towards substitution for cream which is then complimented with the Rice Bran Oil, so in general it can be used with a ratio of 4 parts tofu to 1 part oil as a substitute for double cream and eggs in soft cakes. This recipe uses coconut flour to make a stiffer mix – but you can miss it out if you like or see the muffin recipe next.

Lemon Tofu Cake

160g silken Tofu
100g caster sugar
40g rice bran oil
1 lemon – zest + juice
25g coconut flour
1 tsp baking powder
160g white spelt flour

Blend the Tofu, sugar, Oil and Lemon together, add the coconut flour and mix well, then add the spelt and baking powder and mix together. Put the mix into a paper lined baking tin and bake for 30 mins at 175C.

Lemon Tofu Muffins

1/2

~~1~~ pack – 360g Silken Tofu
80g caster sugar
2 Unwaxed Lemons,
Grate the lemon rind, and add the juice and fruit pulp.
40g Rice Bran Oil.

Put all the above ingredients into the blender and blend till smooth, put 200g white spelt flour and 10g baking powder into a mixing bowl and mix well. Pour in the mixture from the blender, and mix together using a hand whisk. Spoon the mixture into muffin cases and bake at 175 for 20 mins.

Seaweed and Oatcakes

Winter Solstice Fruit Pies

Take a half pound (225g of dried raisins, and soak these for at least 3 days in a mixture of Orange Juice, Lemon Juice, and Rum according to taste. Miss out the rum for children. Best is when the raisins have become plump again.

You can vary this recipe to suit, but basically take a half dozen medium apples, peel them if you wish, and chop into a pan with a little apple juice, add the raisins, some chopped stem ginger, and cinnamon. Cook till the apples have softened and browned.

Make shortcrust pastry using 125g spelt flour, 15g Rice Bran Oil, and 25g sugar and a teaspoon of baking powder. Rub the dry ingredients together then add 50ml cold water and combine using a pastry knife. Roll between 2 sheets of baking paper to get a really thin crust. Using two different cutters, one for the tops, and the other for the bases. Use a pastry brush or piece of kitchen paper, or a small piece of net curtain to oil the tart tin using nut oil or rice bran oil. First cut all the tops using the smaller cutter and put these aside, then cut the bases and put these straight into the tart tin.

Put a good teaspoon of fruit mixture into each base before covering with a lid. Bake at 175C for 20 mins.

Seaweed and Oatcakes

Thank You for reading this book, I hope you found some interesting new ideas in it. For me it has been a considerable amount of work over a long period. It would not have been possible without the help and encouragement of a large number of people.

Special thanks go to Maire Devlin for the photos, proof reading, and tasting of constant recipe revisions. Thanks to the staff at New leaf wholefoods for being willing tasters. Also thanks to Roddy Martine for encouragement editing and proof reading.

This book is dedicated to the army of protestors fighting for our planet. To the protestors in the fracking fields of Fylde, and to the protestors on the Dakota oil and gas pipelines. There is no second planet when the greedy have destroyed this one so please look after it better.

And finally special thanks to Biddles books for making this project affordabe.

Thank You.